# Social Media

*Effective Strategies For Dominating Social Media Marketing with Facebook, Twitter, YouTube, Instagram, LinkedIn, and Pinterest*

2nd Edition

By

Richard Harrison

© Copyright 2015 by – Richard Harrison – All rights reserved.

This document is geared towards providing exact and reliable information in regards to the topic and issue covered. The publication is sold with the idea that the publisher is not required to render accounting, officially permitted, or otherwise, qualified services. If advice is necessary, legal or professional, a practiced individual in the profession should be ordered.

- From a Declaration of Principles which was accepted and approved equally by a Committee of the American Bar Association and a Committee of Publishers and Associations.

In no way is it legal to reproduce, duplicate, or transmit any part of this document in either electronic means or in printed format. Recording of this publication is strictly prohibited and any storage of this document is not allowed unless with written permission from the publisher. All rights reserved.

The information provided herein is stated to be truthful and consistent, in that any liability, in terms of inattention or otherwise, by any usage or abuse of any policies, processes, or directions contained within is the solitary and utter responsibility of the recipient reader. Under no circumstances will any legal responsibility or blame be held against the publisher for any reparation, damages, or monetary loss due to the information herein, either directly or indirectly.

Respective authors own all copyrights not held by the publisher.

The information herein is offered for informational purposes solely, and is universal as so. The presentation of the information is without contract or any type of guarantee assurance.

The trademarks that are used are without any consent, and the publication of the trademark is without permission or backing by the trademark owner. All trademarks and brands within this book are for clarifying purposes only and are the owned by the owners themselves, not affiliated with this document.

# Table of Contents

Introduction .................................................................................. 1

Chapter 1: Why Use Social Media to Promote your Business ............ 3

Chapter 2: Using Facebook to Market your Business ...................... 15

Chapter 3: Ways to Use Twitter to Market your Company ............... 27

Chapter 4: Tips on Using Instagram to Market your Products ......... 37

Chapter 5: Using Pinterest to Market your Products ...................... 51

Chapter 6: Using YouTube for Marketing ........................................ 55

Chapter 7: Using Snapchat for Quick Marketing Tactics ................. 59

Chapter 8: Using Vine for Viral Marketing ...................................... 63

Chapter 9: Using Blogs to Market your Product .............................. 65

Conclusion ................................................................................... 69

# Introduction

I want to thank you and congratulate you for purchasing the book, "Social Media: Effective Strategies For Dominating Social Media Marketing with Facebook, Twitter, YouTube, Instagram, LinkedIn, and Pinterest".

This book contains helpful information about how to use social media to promote your business and boost your sales! The information in this book will help you to create and grow a strong social media presence for your business that will allow you to obtain the all the potential that social media has to offer.

Social Media is being highly adopted by the wider population therefore it is imperative to deliver the right message to the right platform. By reading and taking action on each chapter, you need to learn how to build your social media presence for you can obtain the full benefits. This book will explain to you tips and techniques that will allow you to successfully increase your sales through Facebook, Twitter, YouTube, and other Social Networking Sites!

Thanks again for purchasing this book, I hope you enjoy it!

# Chapter 1

# Why Use Social Media to Promote your Business

The advent of the internet changed the business landscape in many ways - from distribution to promotion. It is not just e-commerce companies that have benefited from the accessibility and convenience of the World Wide Web. Even traditional and brick-and-mortar shops can take advantage of the Internet in order to increase sales and widen their market reach.

Advertising and marketing on the Internet comes in many forms. Banner and pop-up ads on website closely mimic real-world ads that are pervasive wherever the target consumer can be found. They are even more sophisticated now and are able to profile users and expose them to focused ads that can take into account their demographics, geographical location, browsing history and other characteristics. Similarly, native advertising is an evolved form of the advertorials that one can find in newspapers and magazines where an advertisement is disguised as a news article or presented as sponsored content to the readers.

Bloggers, and more recently, vloggers (i.e., YouTube stars) are able to sustain their businesses through sponsored posts. Their followers are easy to categorize and the most popular ones have millions of followers all over the world. This makes companies highly interested in getting exposure through them. Such a marketing tactic is a contemporary version of the testimonial. Consumers are more receptive to products that celebrities and other so-called "experts in the field" are endorsing. However, many consumers also consider bloggers as average people and their testimonials are often perceived to be more genuine and honest in comparison to celebrities who were paid millions of dollars to promote a product. Nonetheless, bloggers are also paid in some form for their promotion.

Many businesses have used social networking sites to market what they have to offer. Social media is another advertising avenue that interests businesses, although many either do not believe in or do not know how to use social networking to its full potential. This is especially true for companies that are already using television, print, radio, out-of-home, activations, and web (in the ways mentioned above). They may find it superfluous or even deem it ineffective. A short Tweet or a Pinterest link that costs zero dollars to create cannot possibly be more effective than a million-dollar TV ad campaign, and that is where less social media savvy marketers are wrong. If you are not yet using social media to promote your business and market your products, then you are definitely missing out on a lot of things.

Here are the most common benefits of using social media to promote your business:

1. Social media enables you to establish or improve brand awareness.

   A vast majority of people visit social networking sites like Twitter, Pinterest, and Facebook regularly. Most users get not only social updates from those websites but also news reports and entertainment. They always check their feeds, with many of them having automatic notifications so they do not miss anything new.

   Getting your brand name all over those social networking sites will help you establish your brand name. It can also strengthen brand recognition and brand awareness. Social networking sites are the best venue that you can use to establish the online presence of your product and your company. Your target consumers will definitely find your brand difficult to miss.

There are many ways to establish brand awareness in the social media. You can create fun YouTube videos that showcase the benefits of your product. You can also use Twitter, Instagram, Pinterest, or Facebook to make your product known to netizens. Many companies create fun and unique online personalities so that they can interact with customers in a more personal way. Others go more serious and corporate. It all depends on the products being sold by the company and the consumer experience that they want customers to have.

2. Social media allows you to check where your competitors stand.

Social media is a great way to keep tabs on your competitors. You can join your competitor's Facebook pages. You can follow them on Twitter and other social media accounts. This will allow you to study how they communicate with their customers.

Avoid using your company's official social media accounts to do this, though. It would also not be good to use an employee's or manager's accounts as these can still be traced to your company. Instead, create dummy accounts that will also allow you to freely message and stealthily follow your competitor's accounts. This is similar to doing competitor analyses by buying and trying the other company's products.

However, it would not be ethical to damage your competitors in any way using social media. This is sometimes done when a company leaves unfavorable and, most likely, fake negative reviews and comments on a competitor's accounts or spreads false information about the competitor all over social media. Netizens are not easy to fool and they can easily verify facts on the internet. By resorting to unethical online tactics, you just might gain a bad reputation that will be difficult to shake off. Remember, anything you put on the Internet will stay there forever.

3. Social media provides a more personalized way of pitching your product.

Social media provides a more personalized approach of promoting or pitching your product. Newspaper ads and television ads seem to be distant and impersonal. Social media is a great venue where you can pitch your products in a more interactive and human way. Most people visit social media to get personal with other people. You can get personal with your potential buyers and potential clients by initiating conversations with them. You can also encourage your existing customers to give you feedback so you will know your improvement points.

However, you should be ready to face both positive and negative feedback from your customers. Not everybody will be 100% satisfied with their product experience, and you should accept that. What is important is how you handle unsatisfied and disgruntled customers. Especially because social media is such a public venue, everyone will be able to see and judge your reactions. Be careful with your use of language and the way you word apologies when they are necessary. Also, it would be best to direct customers to discuss matters privately with your representatives through the proper channels. (See number 8 for further discussion on customer service.)

4. Social media helps you build client trust and loyalty.

Communicating with your clients in a more personal fashion will make them feel important and secure. It will make them feel valued. This will help them build their trust and confidence in your company and your product. This will also improve your customer feedback and it will increase the chances of customer recommendations.

Usually, receiving auto generated e-mails and messages makes customers feel like you do not care enough about their concerns to personally address these. It makes it seem like you are just a corporate entity out to get their money. Personalized social media responses show that there are actual humans behind the company who care and appreciate their customers. However, it is important to give employees handling the social media accounts proper training so that they know how to interact with consumers in the best way possible.

Many corporate social media scandals are usually attributed to "interns" or "junior, low-level officers" who suggest that they do not have the right experience to post properly on social media. It is really not as simple as when you are posting status updates or photos on your personal accounts. Companies have to keep an image that customers can trust and one simple mistake on Twitter or Instagram can break this trust.

Make sure that you have someone trained and qualified who will handle your social media accounts. Depending on the company's organizational structure and culture, you can also have a chain of approvals before a post goes live. At least, have one other person to sign off or review an image or message before it reaches the Internet. Anybody can make a mistake from overlooked grammatical errors that entirely change the meaning of a message to Photoshop disasters. The problem with making a mistake on a company's social media account is that it will be linked to the company itself. This can lead to a devastating change in your relationship with your customers.

5. Social media helps showcase all your products.

It is much easier and costs less to showcase your services and products with social media. You can post photos of your new products online. You can also post any promotions on products or services that you offer.

What is great about social media is that consumers receive your updates in real-time, so they are quickly informed about the latest news about your products. If you simply upload new products or launch promotions on your official website without announcing it in some way, then nobody will know about them. You can definitely announce it in the paper, but most people now receive their news via the Internet. You can also have large billboards on the highways, but some people may miss them on their daily commute or see them too late. The beauty of social media is that information is instant. You can take advantage of this for flash sales or limited edition products.

Some people also find it better to know what they are looking for before going out to buy your product in the shops. Showcasing your products on social media sites makes it easier for them to scrutinize the specifications and see your range of choices. The formats of these sites are also user-friendly so consumers can quickly browse through the selections and check out prices and even reviews by other buyers. Be sure to update regularly. Most people are more inclined to follow businesses that post often and give special deals to their followers.

6. Social media make it easier for you to do market research.

Social media will help you listen to what your existing and potential customers say about your products and about the industry that you are currently in. People are more outspoken when they are on social networking sites. They are more honest and critical. This will allow you to discover what your customers really think of your product. You can gain a lot of consumer insights and reviews just by taking a look at what people are saying.

The Internet allows people to have an audience who can hear their thoughts and insights, so it is important to monitor any mentions of your products, brand and company to get an idea of how people feel about them. Turning on Google Alerts can help you as well as tracking hashtags. It is important to use the right tags and keywords for your own posts that people can also use. You can also take a look at what is trending and if your posts are going viral - whether positively or negatively.

It is much easier to solicit information about consumer experiences through social media because of its convenience. A comment or dislike is simpler to do than writing a proper e-mail, filling up forms or calling a hotline. You can also give incentives to people posting about your products or reposting your own posts. This encourages people to share about their experience. It also shows that you value your consumers as a part of the development of your products and brand. Many will appreciate this and it creates brand loyalty.

7. You can use social networking sites to strengthen your customer service.

Social networking sites allow you to answer the customer's concerns and questions in a timely manner. This will increase customer satisfaction. Social media is also one of the most inexpensive ways to serve your customers.

However, remember to switch to more private channels when handling delicate matters. It is not good to have a long Twitter exchange about a customer's problem that everyone can see. You may have other users adding to the conversation, leading to the whole thing blowing up and being a bigger issue than it actually is. Conversely, you should not simply ignore complaints and concerns that people are posting.

Only give public responses that will be useful to your general consumer base like guidelines on product use or information on how to contact your business. These details will be helpful to everyone, but for more specific concerns, send the user a private message or ask them for other contact details so you can communicate with them and resolve their issue.

Even though social media sites are quite casual venues, it is still important to maintain your image and show that you take all your clients seriously. Giving sardonic or even slightly joking responses may backfire on you. Treat every consumer with respect and your brand will gain the same in return.

8. You can use social networking sites to establish yourself as an expert and showcase your talents.

If you are a life coach, fitness coach, lawyer, or an accountant, social networking sites will help you establish yourself as an expert in your field. It is a great way to show off your knowledge and expertise on a certain subject. This will help you get more clients and it will help build your reputation.

You can also do this for your company. Aside from sales-driven posts, you can post about topics related to your line of business. These should be informative and interesting to your consumers, but these do not necessarily have to direct them to purchase your products. This technique helps present you as a reliable and exciting source of information. More users will also follow you if you do not always just post about selling your products. Giving people an assortment of posts on different topics will help guard against fatigue from your social media presence.

You may and should post as often as possible, perhaps several times a day, but give variety. Be funny and trendy so that more people will relate to your brand. That will also encourage users to repost and share your content with their friends and followers.

9. Social media enables you to enhance your personal relationships and expand your business contacts.

It can do this by helping you reconnect with old friends who can help your business. It can also help generate marketing leads. LinkedIn is great for business networking. You don't only discover people in similar fields, but you also read highly credible posts on important business topics. Join groups and be active on forums. These features are not available to people without accounts on the site, so having one will be important and will also help you establish yourself in your field.

You should follow people whom you find inspiring. Social networking sites help you connect with other professionals and other business owners who may be interested to collaborate with you. This is especially important for young businessmen and startups since they can greatly benefit from the guidance of veterans. This will also help them find potential partners, sponsors and even investors.

As such, make sure that your online image is impeccably positive and professional. You can even have a separate professional and personal account on different social media websites, or you can take advantage of privacy settings. Always take time to consider and review your material before you post any content. Make sure that you do not put anything on the Internet that can be considered offensive or scandalous to any individuals or groups of people. Your business contacts and consumers can easily trace these back to you.

Also, make sure to keep yourself and your co-workers or employees well-informed and up-to-date with what is appropriate in today's times. What was considered polite a few years ago may no longer be politically correct now. It is as well easy to make a cultural faux pas especially when dealing with foreign cultures in the development of your products or interactions with consumers.

10. Social media gives you free advertising.

It costs nothing to have a verified account on most social media websites. You can post as many ads and promotions as you want without having to spend a cent.

For more advanced marketing, you can do targeted sponsored ads, but this may not be cost-effective for new businesses or those with niche markets.

If you take into consideration how much ads cost per click or per pixel, then you will be able to better appreciate the accessibility of using social media for advertising. It is also much less expensive than buying your own domain and designing a website, although it is still good to maintain an official website with your own URL.

Now that you have an understanding of the benefits on why you should be using social media for your business. Let us begin the process by first looking at the most popular social media platform Facebook to get you started.

# Chapter 2

# Using Facebook to Market your Business

Facebook is, hands down, the most popular social networking site in the world today. Facebook has 1.23 billion active users and about 757 billion members use this social networking site daily. An average American spends at least 45 minutes every day on the site. This is the reason why it is a great idea to use Facebook to promote your business. Facebook gives you an instant audience.

Facebook has many business and marketing benefits, including:

1. Facebook is an amazing low-cost promotion and marketing strategy.

   Marketing campaigns can cost thousands of dollars. But, you can do these marketing activities and campaigns on Facebook for a fraction of the cost incurred in other marketing channels. Facebook is one of the best marketing platforms for small and medium scale businesses.

   Large companies can also try to use their marketing concepts on Facebook first before committing to a large scale marketing campaign.

   You can post limitless content and images that promote your products and explain what your company is all about. When posting content, make sure that it is not too complicated and it is easy to read. Take note that most users check Facebook on mobile devices, so it would not be comfortable to read long posts that are poorly formatted. Use bullet points, albeit sparingly, and be succinct with the way you state your message.

Headlines are also important as these are the first things that people see on their feeds. Keep them short enough to not get cut when seen on a feed. For images, use good quality images. It is not necessary to use high resolution photos on social media, especially when Facebook already compresses images before posting. Just make sure that they do not appear pixelated as that may look unprofessional and cheap.

2. Facebook is a great venue to publicize your business name.

You can build brand recognition through Facebook. Facebook is a great place for you to publicize your business name, contact details, address, and product description. You can also publicize stories about the history and your staff. These stories could create interest in your company and your products. This helps people connect with your company and understand what your core values are.

Through Facebook, you can also give people updates on things you are working on. This can be new features, products or promos. By following you on Facebook, your loyal customers will be the first ones to know about these updates. This is even more effective than advertising on paper, on TV or on the radio.

Make sure that all your posts carry your brand name and trademarks to aid in recognition and recall of consumers. Your branding does not need to shout; subtle but repetitive branding is the key. Frequent posting will also help keep you in the mind of your customers. Be strategic with your timing.

For instance, if you are offering a breakfast product, then post around breakfast time. If you have a holiday promo, start promoting around the holidays.

As much as possible, be purposeful with your posts. Some companies just like posting for no reason at all. What is unfortunate is that their followers may get annoyed and stop following them because their posts are of no value to them or are timed very poorly.

3. Facebook enables you to communicate with your potential and existing customers.

You can use Facebook to communicate with potential and existing clients by posting a status. You can also share videos and pictures from your business. Creating informative Facebook posts is a great way to share interesting information to your existing and potential clients.

When you use other marketing channels like TV, print, radio and even some forms of web advertising, you tend to be doing the *shotgun approach*. This means that you just keep on shooting randomly, hoping to somehow hit a target. So, you communicate to a wide audience with the intention of capturing a small number of potential customers. This can prove to be costly and inefficient. When you use Facebook for marketing, you are doing the *rifle approach*. You shoot once and already hit the target. This is because your followers are either already existing customers or people who are interested in your product offerings. There is no need to look for them because they are already within your reach.

Also, your followers usually share similar profiles and characteristics with their own Facebook friends. So, by sharing your content, they are effectively doing targeted marketing for you. Also, most people will share Facebook posts that they think their friends will also find interesting; hence, make sure that your posts lend themselves well to being shared. Ensure that branding will remain intact and unaltered.

4. You can use Facebook for customer support.

Your clients can post "after-sales" questions on your FB wall and your staff or customer support representatives can answer your customers from there. This method is often more efficient and more cost-effective than answering consumer questions through phone calls, although, this can also be a double-edged sword. It may make contacting customer service easier for clients and help you address concerns in a speedier manner.

5. Facebook can help raise your brand awareness through positive word of mouth.

You can increase your brand's reputation by encouraging potential and existing customers to hit the like button. Facebook can also help increase your website traffic. Be sure to provide links to your other social media accounts and to your official website. Social media presence also helps in search engine optimization. The more content there is on the web about your company and products, the more search engines will favor your website when it comes to listing results to keyword searches. You should be consistent and strategic with your keywords and branding triggers.

Here are some tips that you can use with Facebook to promote your product and increase your sales:

- Set up a business page.

The first thing that you should do when starting your marketing campaign through Facebook is to set up your business page. Remember that your Facebook page represents your business. It works like your business card, website, and promo material.

You have to remember that businesses that have a Facebook page are automatically included in the Facebook "places" function. This allows customers and client to "check in" on their mobile devices when they visit your store. This will increase the popularity and visibility of your Facebook page.

Make sure that your images look good and are representative of your brand. Do not forget to give an informative write-up about your company in the about section. Also, make sure that all your contact details are correct and that any website links are functional. A lot of people do seek businesses out on Facebook out of instinct, so they should also find you there.

- Build up your followers.

You have to drive as many people as possible to your Facebook page by encouraging them to "like" your page. A percentage of Facebook visitors can be converted to actual customers. You can also increase your Facebook followers by promoting your Facebook page in your marketing material, in your store, in newsletters, email signatures, and your websites. You can also integrate or create a link directing to your Facebook page on your other social networking accounts such as Instagram and Twitter.

You can also increase your followers through paid ads and sponsored stories which will be targeted to certain interests, demographics, and geographic areas. Your partners can also post your links on their own accounts with the aim to encourage their followers to "like" your page.

- Launch Facebook contests.

Everyone wants to have free stuff. Contests often attract potential new clients. It is also a good way to communicate the benefits and superiority of your products. Facebook contests usually become viral. With a little promo work, your fan base will rise dramatically.

The mechanics of your contests may include liking your page, inviting friends to follow you, or generally spreading information about your company. Make the reward enticing and remember to spread the word about the contest to as many people as possible.

Examples of Facebook contests can be photo contests that can be won by the number of likes, story writing contests judged by your team members, or simply reposting content on their own pages.

However, you must take into consideration Facebook's updated terms on launching contests on their platform. Avoid violating any of their rules.

- Have a clear Facebook marketing goal and strategy.

It is important to have a clear goal and marketing strategy when you are using Facebook to market the product. How many "likes" or Facebook subscribers do you want to have? Do you want your Facebook page to generate at least 10% of your total annual sales?

Aside from having a Facebook marketing goal, you also have to create a marketing strategy which may include the following items:

- Posting a daily photo featuring customers who use the product. This will instantly make the clients feel good and it will entice potential clients.

- Encouraging your clients to post their photos while they are in your store.
- Creating a post every day about a feature product.

- Communicate with your users using a "human voice".

Facebook users want to feel that they are talking to actual person. If you want to engage your Facebook subscriber, you have to communicate with them with a "human voice". You have to write posts that are likeable and relatable. Do not write business jargons or write boring posts about company processes. Instead, appeal to the human voice.

Some companies opt to have a fictional brand personality that people can interact with. These are like online mascots that both encapsulate what their brand is all about and are also relatable to their audience. They should have names, faces and personalities that are similar to real people. They can be adopted from existing brand images or created as a sort of customer support character.

Make sure that any characters you create are not potentially offensive to anyone. Their online behavior should also be consistent, so make sure that the people behind them are trained well. You can consider them as puppet masters who make the character come to life.

- Post regularly.

Social networking sites like Facebook are built around frequent updates. Recent studies show that around 50% of Facebook users check their Facebook Newsfeed at least once a day. So, it is important to post something on your Facebook page at least once daily. But, do not post anything for the sake of posting. You have to post only when you come up with something interesting. Remember that your status posts must be valuable, or at least relevant, to your subscribers.

You can assign someone on your team or hire someone as a social media manager who can manage all your accounts including your Facebook account. He or she would have to plot all the planned posts on a schedule that should be followed. It is not good to post sporadically. You must really think of the best time to post to get as much exposure as possible. For instance, you would not want to post when most of the customers in your time zone are sleeping as even the most avid Facebook checkers would miss those posts.

Some studies suggest early mornings or during work breaks like at lunch or in mid-afternoon, although it is best to conduct your own research on your market to find out what will work best for your company and marketing needs.

- Post videos and pictures.

It is important to post pictures and videos regularly. Videos and pictures are more engaging than texts. These videos and pictures will keep your subscribers interested and entertained.

For example:

- A clothing company can post photos of their new stocks and products.

- A personal trainer may post videos of a new exercise routine.

- An architect may post pictures of a house that he is working on.

- A software company may post instructional videos on how to use the latest software feature.

However, make sure that your pictures are easy to view on most devices. For instance, infographics are usually capable of relaying information better than a long article. However, some infographics are too long and have poor formatting, so people just scroll past them on their feeds. Be mindful of good design. For social media, minimalist layouts usually work best and translate on different types of screens well.

For videos, make sure to spend time and effort on good production. Set aside resources for a proper shoot and processing. Though it can be done and may work for some concepts, shooting on a low quality camera (like a camera phone) without much thought into what you are doing may not produce professional results. If you find video shoots too complicated, you can opt for animated videos that can convey your intended message. You can also simply outsource your video production to a third party company.

Treat your videos as if they were television ads. Many companies think that producing videos for the Internet means that they can get away with a lower quality. You are still a business and you have to show that you value excellence in everything you do.

- Conduct surveys.

You can use Facebook to conduct surveys. You can conduct surveys to determine customer satisfaction and customer preference. There are online survey applications that you can use that are compatible with Facebook or that you can link to from your page. Do not just ask people to leave comments. It is better if they were to fill out proper online forms with results that you can automatically generate. That will make it easier for you to analyze responses and generate conclusions.

It is also good to give people a reward for accomplishing a survey. This can be in the form of free product samples or promo codes. They will take it more seriously that way.

You can also do targeted surveys by inviting particular individuals to be respondents. You can focus on a particular age group, location, or interests based on their profiles. Make them feel special by getting selected to be a part of your survey.

- Try out the Sponsored Stories service on Facebook.

Facebook has recently launched a new form of advertising called "sponsored stories". The ads will be displayed on the Newsfeed of the friends of the people who "liked" your business or fan page. Sponsored stories will ensure that your Facebook activity will be prominent. The ads contain actual activity and not just a generic marketing or advertising copy. They are considered to not be as intrusive as Facebook banner ads and are usually not flagged by ad blocking applications. It is also believed that more people will click on them than other forms of more overt online ads.

- Answer Facebook inquiries in a timely manner.

You have to build a strong relationship with your subscribers. One way to do this is to answer their inquiries in a timely manner. Engage sincerely with your subscribers.

You can hire someone to man your Facebook account during office hours or, if possible, round-the-clock 24/7. Even comments that just say "Thank you" should not be ignored.

## SOCIAL MEDIA

Thank them back for their appreciation. Do not leave any inquiries hanging as this can frustrate some customers and make them leave negative comments.

- Use Facebook Insights to get to know your existing and potential clients.

Facebook Insights can help you learn more about the users who like your page. You can tailor your posts and offers to meet the needs and interests of your subscribers.

- Celebrate your milestones with your Facebook fans.

One of the powerful ways to strengthen your relationship with your Facebook fans is to celebrate your milestones with them even if it is something small.

- Ask the right questions.

One way to engage your users is to ask entertaining and interesting questions. If done right, asking the right questions can increase for Facebook fan base and it can build a great relationship with your current subscribers.

- Do not hard sell.

When you are using Facebook to promote your products, you have to try your best not to hard sell. Hard selling will annoy your subscribers.

- Encourage feedback.

Smart companies tap their Facebook followers to get instant ideas and feedback on their new product design and their customer service. Facebook is a great and inexpensive way of generating customer feedback.

- Stay on Topic

People who "like" your business page expect your posts to be related to your industry and your brand. You can post the following:

- Write about current events related to your brand or your industry.

- Ask your audience to post stories and pictures about your brand on your wall.

- Repost interesting contents about your brand or your industry.

- Find and share funny and entertaining videos that are closely related to your industry or brand. For example, if you are running a yoga studio, you can post funny pet yoga videos. If you are running a gym, post funny and entertaining exercise videos.

You have to remember that "unliking" a page is just as easy as "liking" a page. A single uninteresting and off-topic post can urge subscribers to unsubscribe to your business page.

You now have a good understanding about Facebook. I encourage you to take action right now and go setup your Facebook page and apply what you learned in this chapter to make your business a success.

# Chapter 3

# Ways to Use Twitter to Market your Company

Twitter is one of the most important social networking sites today. Twitter has around 280 million active users. Around 500 million tweets are posted every day.

Twitter has a number of benefits for your business. Twitter is one of the social networking sites that you can use to communicate with your followers.

Twitter is also used to generate leads and attract new customers. It is also a great way to liven the image of your brand. This powerful social networking site is also one the most effective ways to promote your product and your brand.

Here are some of the ways that you can use Twitter to market your product and your company:

1. Identify your purpose for creating a Twitter account.

Before you create a Twitter account for your business, you have to identify your purpose. Are you using your Twitter account to generate leads? Are you using your Twitter account to build your brand? Are you using your Twitter account to share information and ideas?

2. You have to ensure that your Twitter account reflects your brand.

When you set up your Twitter account, you have to make sure that your brand reflects your brand. You can do this by doing the following:

- Your Twitter name should be your brand name – This tip is pretty obvious. But, it's surprising that many businesses actually do not use their brand name in creating their products. Most businesses use a cute or witty Twitter name that is not related to their business. This is actually a wrong move! Twitter names are usually referred to as "Twitter handles" and are signified by a "@" symbol. When coming up with your name, take into consideration how it will look as a handle. For example, Mark and Stacey's Surfers Shop would read as "@markandstaceyssurfersshop".

  Notice how the format makes the name difficult to read and even somewhat changes the branding. A better handle would be simply "@markandstaceys". You can also consider using an underscore as in "@surfer_shop" if the phrase "Surfer Shop" can easily be associated with the brand anyway.

- Use your company logo as your Twitter photo – Many businesses do not recognize the importance of using your business logo as your company photo. Using your logo as your Twitter photo gives you an instant opportunity to market your product. Also, take into consideration that your profile photo usually appears as a small icon, so intricate logos will lose details. For example, if your logo has a tagline beneath it, then people will no longer be able to read the tagline. You can opt to use a simplified version of your logo instead. Twitter profiles also allow you to upload a banner photo. You can use larger images for that.

- Also, get your account verified. There may be users who will sign up on Twitter pretending to be you, a representative of your company, or your company's official Twitter account. This can lead to a public relations disaster, especially if the account was created to damage your reputation. A verified Twitter account has a blue check beside the name. This is a privilege that celebrities and businesses take advantage of as they are the ones most vulnerable to fake accounts being created under their name. Contact Twitter on how you can get verified as their policies change. They will require you to send them an application for verification.

3. Define your Twitter strategy.

It is important to define your Twitter strategy. Do you want to communicate more information to your Twitter followers or do you want to listen to their ideas and feedback? If your goal is to influence other people and promote or sell your product, your Twitter strategy must be communication-based. You have to attract attention. To do this, you have to tweet often. You also need to send direct messages, and engage more Twitter users.

If your goal is to learn about your potential customers, perform market analysis, or provide customer service to your clients, your Twitter strategy should be to listen. In this case, you have to use Twitter filtering tools like Twitter lists and hashtags.

4. Tweet at least ten times a day to keep your brand name visible on the Twitter Newsfeed.

It is important to tweet at least ten tweets every day. Your tweet can contain links to your website or some relevant resource. Take a look at the tweets of your competitors and other accounts with a lot of followers to get inspiration on how you can be interesting and worth following on Twitter.

5. Create a certain Twitter persona that your audience can relate to.

If you want to capture the interest of your audience, you have to create a persona that your clients can relate to. You have to create a brand personality that your clients could certainly relate to. There are five major types of brand personality: sincerity, excitement, ruggedness, competence, and sophistication. You can choose which type of brand personality you want to adopt, so all your Tweets should sound like they are something your brand personality would actually say.

6. Find your keywords.

If you are using your Twitter account for marketing purposes, you might want to use the Google Keyword Planner to find the right keywords that make up your market or your niche. You need to tap into existing marketing traffic. It is not a wise idea to build traffic from scratch. It is best to identify the existing keywords that your existing and potential customers use to find your product.

7. Identify your hashtags.

## SOCIAL MEDIA

A hashtag is a tool used to make a word more searchable. You need to place a # before a word to create a hashtag. Hashtags allow subscribers to tap into conversations in Twitter. Hashtags will help you discover the trending conversations among Twitter users. Hashtags will help you identify and connect with people who may be interested in your products and your services.

Remember that it is important to use a maximum of 2 hashtags per tweet. Using a hashtag is a great way to ensure that you are communicating with people who are actually interested about your brand, product, or the topic that you are interested about. But, using too many hashtags is annoying and overwhelming. As with Twitter handles, opt for hashtags that are short and readable.

There are many tools that you can use in researching for hashtags, including:

- Twitter Toolbar- You can search keywords, terms, or people by using the toolbar located at the top right page on Twitter. For example, if you are a soap manufacturer, you can find conversations about soap by typing #soap in the Twitter search field.
- Hashtags.org – Hashtags.org help businesses with their research needs. This organization also helps people with their social networking strategies.
- Twitter Reach
- Topsy
- Social Mention

8. Promote your Twitter ID in your other social networking accounts.

Publish your Twitter ID on your other social media accounts and communications. It is a good idea to include your Twitter ID in your email signature. You can also publish your Twitter ID on your Facebook account and on your website. One way to build your Twitter following is to start with your current clients and other people you know.

9. Use Twitter tools like Tweepi and Insightpool to target people who may want to follow you.

The best way to build your Twitter network is to create a content that targets people who may be interested to "follow" you. You can use tools like Tweepi, Insightpool, Twtrland, and Twitonomy to target interested Twitter users.

10. Follow the "follow first" rule.

When you follow people on Twitter, they are most likely interested in following you. The "follow first" rule is one of the great ways to gain followers. Remember that every account can only follow up to 2000 users, so choose to follow the ones who are more likely to be interested in following your account.

Do not fall for offers that claim that they can gain you more followers in a short period of time. What usually happens is that your account will be followed by dummy accounts that are not maintained by actual users. That will not gain you any leads. Even though it may look good that the number of your followers is quite high, that number can quickly diminish when Twitter cleans up these dummy accounts.

11. Follow the "offer-following" rule.

You can gain Twitter followers by offering something to the users in exchange of following your Twitter account. You can give away some valuable information or an ebook. It is important to note that you have to give something that is valuable to your audience. Also, make it easy for your followers to claim their rewards.

12. Follow the "favorites-follower" rule.

13. Find Tweets that match your targeted keywords and your interests. Favorite these tweets and usually, these Twitter users will return the favor by following your Twitter account. This will give you more engaged and high quality followers. Research first before you tweet.

It is very crucial to research first before you post something on Twitter. You have to make sure that your tweets are accurate and interesting. There are lots of false information floating around on the Internet. It is especially easy to fall for something that many people are hyping. Case in point, many users fall for "celebrity Twitter deaths" where tweets about the supposed death of a famous personality are shared until the news of the death starts trending. Many of these would eventually be proven to be false.

14. Create original content that serves your purpose.

Your tweets have to be original, interesting and engaging. It must also serve your purpose. Write about product updates or industry news. You can also tweet links that direct your Twitter followers to the most recent posts on your blog or your website.

15. Resend tweets.

Social media marketing experts agree that you have to send a tweet at least four times to cover the different time zones. But, of course, you have to resend the tweets in different angles. You can mix the word up or restructure your sentences.

16. Schedule your tweets.

Studies show that the best time to post tweets if you want to be retweeted is Friday at 4 p.m. Eastern Standard Time.

There are applications that you can use to schedule your tweets like the Buffer App Tool. You can also use Buffer's Analytic tab to monitor your Twitter engagement.

17. Retweet great content.

One of the things that you can do is to retweet great content. Doing this will help you accomplish two things:

- It shows your Twitter followers that you are an active member of the community.
- It helps you make friends with other Twitter influencers.
- You can also re-tweet posts about your products that other users have tweeted about. Some users will tweet about business just hoping that they will re-tweet or favorite the post.

18. Repost your tweets on your Facebook and other social media accounts.

It is best to repost your tweets on your Facebook and other social media accounts when it is appropriate.

19. Check if your Twitter marketing strategy is working.

It is important to check where you stand on social media tools such as:

- Kred.com
- WeFollow.com
- Peerindex.com
- Klout.com

Klout.com is one of the most popular tools that you can use to check your influence on Twitter and other social networking sites.

It is now time for you to take action on setting up your business twitter account if you do not already have one. If you find that sending out 10 tweets at the beginning might be to much for right now, you must send out at least 5 tweets a day to get into the habit and gradually build up to 10 tweets. This way you will get your brand out there.

# Chapter 4

# Tips on Using Instagram to Market your Products

Instagram is a great way to promote your products and your services. Instagram will help you promote your products and services for free. Here are some of the things that you can do to boost your sales and increase brand awareness through Instagram:

1. Create an Instagram account for your business.

    It is quite easy to create an Instagram account for your business. All you need to do is:

    - Download Instagram and sign up. All you need is an e-mail. Instagram works on most mobile devices, so be sure that you will be able to use the app on your device of choice. It would be good to have both Android and Apple devices in different screen sizes (i.e., smartphone and tablet) so that you can check how your posts look on those screens. Sometimes, the interface looks different on different mobile platforms. Also, though not a lot of users check Instagram on their desktop, it is possible to see Instagram pages on Internet browsers. Be sure to check how your page looks on different browsers, too.

    - It is important to choose a username that represents your business and your brand. If your brand name is already taken, pick a username that reflects your business. As with Twitter, be mindful of how it would look as a handle with a "@" symbol. It is also possible to use underscores in your username. Make sure that it is not too long and is easy to read.

- Add a biography, profile photo, and a link to your website. This will help you increase brand recognition. It is not possible to link to any websites on Instagram except in your bio, so make sure that you link to your official website there. If you do not have a website, then it would be best to have the URL to one of your other social media accounts. It is best to use your company logo as your Instagram profile photo. Take note that Instagram profile photos show up as circle icons, so the sides or corners of your photo may get cropped. Keep important elements of your profile photo such as the brand name and logo in the middle of the photo you upload to prevent them from being cropped out.

- Link your Instagram account to your Facebook and your other social networking site accounts. When you post something on Instagram, the followers on your other social media accounts will be able to see it instantly.

- You can also place Instagram plug-ins on your website where slideshows or feeds of photos from your account will be displayed on the page. This is especially good for companies and professionals who rely heavily on images for their businesses such as design studios or photographers.

## SOCIAL MEDIA

- Announce in your Facebook page or other social networking site that you have an Instagram account. Ask your Twitter followers and Facebook fans to follow your Instagram account.

2. Create an Instagram tab on your company's Facebook page.

   Creating an Instagram tab of your Facebook page enables you to instantly share your photos on Instagram to your Facebook followers. You can easily do this by logging into your Facebook account. Then, access your Facebook page. Search for "Instagram" in the search bar at the top of the window. Select "Instagram feed" under the section for "Apps". Install the application for your page and set the proper permissions so that Facebook can access your Instagram feed. InstaTab is another app that you can use and it displays photos in a grid layout.

   Big companies like Mercedes Benz are very intelligent and brilliant at linking their Instagram content on their Facebook accounts.

3. Post creative photos of your products and services.

   Instagram allows you to post creative photos of your products and services. It is a very image-heavy platform. Instagram also allows you to showcase your products and services through striking photos. For example, if you own a coffee shop, you can post photos of your daily specials. If you own an online clothing company, you can post photos of your clothes. If you own an architecture firm, you can post photos of your latest projects.

   But, be careful in using Instagram to showcase your products and services. Limit your Instagram post to three posts a day. Spamming pictures will not help you increase brand trust and recognition. In fact, it will annoy your Instagram followers and it may drive them to unfollow you.

4. Create an Instagram brand specific strategy.

    You have to keep your Instagram content focused on how you want your clients perceive your brand. Connect your brand with your Instagram 'tribe' in a consistent and in a visual way.

    Create a style and signature that you can recreate on all your posts so that they are unique to brand and memorable to your followers. Doing so will also make you stand out from other Instagram accounts. This can be a design choice for your photos or the use of similar filters.

5. Use hashtags in your Instagram posts.

    As mentioned earlier in this book, hashtags will make your posts more searchable. You can actually use as many hashtags as you like because you are not limited by character count. But, using too many can be irritating, annoying, and visually confusing. It is best to use a maximum of 2 hashtags. Make sure that your hashtags are relevant to your company, products and market. Some people use unrelated hashtags in a comical way, but that is not advisable to do for businesses.

    Think of hashtags as a way for customers searching for products or services to find what they are looking for in a more convenient manner. You can also use hashtags to find posts by other users that are related to your business. You can use the search function to search for both users and hashtags.

6. Utilize brand-specific hashtags.

It is best to include your brand name in your hashtags. Also, it will be helpful to use unique tags for certain marketing campaigns that you are currently running. For example, if one of your products is "on sale", create a unique hashtag for the campaign. For example, you can use #summersale2014, #50percentoffonallitems #pricecut2014.

You can also use engaging brand specific hashtags. For example, if you are selling alcoholic drinks, you can use the hashtag #drinkdifferent. Of course, this hashtag is a pun of the popular Apple tagline "Think Different". If you are selling burger patties, you can use the hashtag #nobunintended. You have to be creative in using hashtags.

7. Use general hashtags.

It will be useful and easier to use general hashtag. For example, if you have a coffee shop, you can post a photo of your specials and include general hashtags like #coffee or you can use hashtags like #cappuccino.

8. Use appropriate trending hashtags.

If you want to ensure that thousands of people will see your post, use a trending hashtag that is appropriate and relevant to your brand.

9. Interact with your Instagram followers.

Be sure to check your Instagram account on a regular basis and respond to customer inquiries right away. This will give you a chance to build a strong relationship with your customers.

Also, check your followers' updates to check if they are posting about you or seeking for products and services that you offer. Leaving comments on other users' posts also gives you exposure. Their followers can see you and check out your account. Seeing how you interact with their friends can also help in building a positive image among your market.

10. Make your followers famous.

Starbucks is one of the top three brands on Instagram. One of their Instagram tactics is to show their appreciation to their customers by sharing their photos on their Instagram and Facebook account. If you spot a customer posting a photo of your product, repost that photo and give a shout out to that particular customer. Your customer will surely appreciate it.

Be sure to ask permission first before reposting and publishing your customer's name and other information (e.g., location, purchase). Some people prefer to stay private and not have their posts shared to a wide audience.

11. Like the photos of your followers.

It would help if you would acknowledge the awesomeness of your followers by liking their photos, especially if they emulate your brand or include your product in their photos. This is the simplest thing you can do to show your appreciation for the people who patronize your business.

12. Respond to all the comments on your posts.

One of the most effective ways to interact with your Instagram followers is to reply to all the comments on your posts. This will make your followers feel like they are engaged to a "human voice".

13. Mention your customers.

Like on Twitter and Facebook, you can mention your followers by using @ before the username. You can say something like, Thank you @customer for trying out our new latte flavor. Do not forget to mention the users you are replying to by including their handles on your comments. For example, you should write "@lisasmith Thanks for the lovely comment!". This will ensure that the original commenter can see your reply. Take note that Instagram does not have a Reply function the way Facebook does.

14. Focus on engaging with your Instagram followers and your customers.

You have to post more than just your brand and your products. You have to authentically and sincerely connect with your followers by posting things that are important to them. For example, if you are selling cabinets, you can post photos that show how your customers can sort out their clothes inside the cabinet. The post is still about your product, but it also caters your customers' needs. It is information that most of your customers could relate to.

15. Enhance your photos.

Spend time in making sure that your Instagram photos are visually appealing. Use photo applications to enhance your image like Adobe Photoshop, Photoshake, or Diptic to edit your photos. Instagram has a built-in camera and photo editing app but its features are quite limited. Here's the list of the other apps that you can use to enhance your image:

- Aviary
- Lens Flare

- PXL
- Tangent App
- DXP Free
- Tilt Shift Generator
- Average Camera Pro
- Everlapse
- 8mm Vintage Camera
- Vintagio
- CrossProcess
- PicFame
- Overgram
- Bokehful
- Slow Shutter Cam
- Snapspeed
- Afterlight
- Pixlr
- VSCO

Take note that Instagram compresses the photos you upload, so you may lose the quality on your photos when you post them. Also, photos must be square so keep them in a 1:1 ratio.

Some professionals and businesses that post on Instagram actually take photos with a high-end camera first before

## SOCIAL MEDIA

editing them. Most camera phones do not produce good enough photos. It will be more convenient, though, to invest in a good smartphone with a camera that you can use. After applying filters and compression, most users cannot really tell the difference between photos taken with a DSLR and a decent camera phone.

Do not go overboard with using too many filters, stickers and texts. Keep your images simple. Although, do make sure that it fits with your brand image. A street wear brand can easily get away with messy graffiti style photos.

16. Post videos.

Instagram allows you to post short videos. Use this feature to showcase your products and events. Instagram videos can last from 3 to 15 seconds. It can also have a sound. Although there are apps that can help you fit in more seconds into a video like with Hyperlapse (which speeds up your videos) or Video Collage (which stitches together several videos into one video).

17. Showcase the practicality of your products.

Use Instagram to showcase the practicality of your products. You can post photos of how your products are used in real life. For example, if you are selling bottled water, you can post a photo of your customers drinking your water at a crowded outdoor concert.

18. You have to showcase your brand and your company's story.

You can post cool and hip photos that represent your brand's history. You can also post something photos that represent your brand's principles, mission, and values. You can also post photos of your employees and staff. You can post photos how you make and ship each product. It is best to also post "behind the scenes" photos.

19. Post fun and authentic photos and videos of your company's CEO.

You have to make the top executives look more personable. This will increase customer engagement. Post quirky and wacky videos and photos and videos of your CEO. For example, you can post a video about what your CEO is doing when he is not working.

20. Share exclusive content to your Instagram followers.

To make your Instagram followers feel special, post photos or content that you have not posted in your other social networking accounts yet.

21. Launch a product on Instagram.

If you are opening a new store or you are launching a new product, it is best to do it live on this amazing photo sharing site. For example, if you are launching a new product, make a video or two showing your preparation for the product launch. This will get your Instagram followers excited. Tease your Instagram followers with a 15 second video showing how you are preparing for the product launch.

22. Show your post product launch clean up or party (if you have one).

This will allow you to show your employees and yourself authentically to your Instagram followers.

## SOCIAL MEDIA

23. Ask your followers to comment on your photos and videos.

You can ask your Instagram followers to comment on your photos and videos by asking open ended questions. You can also use the phrase "let us know what you guys think" after every post.

24. Partner with other Instagram brands.

Instagram is a great tool to use to partner with other brands and companies. You can ask companies to post about your brand and in return, you can also make an Instagram post about their brands. For example, if you are selling sunglasses, you can partner up with companies that sell SPF lotions. If you are selling rubber shoes, you can partner up with companies that sell sports socks.

25. Ask your Instagram followers to create a caption your posts.

One way to engage your customers and Instagram followers is to post a hip photo of your products and then ask your followers to make a caption. Your followers will definitely have a lot of fun captioning it. You can also create a photo caption contest and give free giveaways to followers who wrote the most interesting and fun captions.

26. Run an Instagram contest.

Running Instagram photo contests is a great way to get user-generated content. It is also a great way to interact with your Instagram followers and customers. Here are some tips that you can use in running an Instagram photo contest:

- Set goals – Like any other great marketing campaign, you have to set goals. This will allow you to monitor your ROI or return on investment. Do you want to generate leads? Do you want to increase sales? Do you want to increase brand awareness?

- Identify your target market – Before you start a photo contest, you have to identify your target market.

- Create your budget – It is necessary to create a certain budget for your photo contest and stick to it. How much are you willing to spend for this contest?

- Choose your prize – It is necessary to choose a prize that will entice your target market to join.

- Choose a contest type – To ensure that your Instagram contest will help you reach your goals; you have to pick a contest type that will capture the interest of your target market. You can run a vote contest, an essay contest, a video contest, a photo contest, a raffle, or a photo caption contest.

- Pick a theme for your contest – If you are running a photo contest, choose a theme that will help you achieve your goals. Also, make sure that your theme will help you generate UGC or User Generated Content. For example, if you have a clothing store pick seasonal themes like Best Summer Outfil Contest or Back to School contest.

- Establish the contest time frame – You have to be clear about the time frame of your contest. The short time frame is best when you want to get fast results.

- Be clear about the contest mechanics – You have to be clear about the contest mechanics. This will prevent disputes, miscommunication, and a decrease in customer satisfaction.

- Promote your Instagram contest – To get as many entries as possible, you have to promote your Instagram contest on your other social networking sites. You can also email your existing customers and ask them to join.

- Feature the winning entry on your website and social networking sites – If you are running a photo contest, it would be best to feature the winning photo on your social networking accounts and your website.

27. Be true to your company and your brand.

You have to ensure that you are being true to your company and your brand. You have to ensure that your photos have a well-defined personality and voice.

28. Share experiences to your Instagram audience.

It is important to share experiences with your Instagram audience. This will establish a strong connection to your Instagram followers and your potential customers.

Instagram is a great way to market your product. It is also an inexpensive way to promote your products and get to know your customers more closely. Apply what you just read this chapter on Instagram to boost your sales and increase your brand recognition.

# Chapter 5

# Using Pinterest to Market your Products

Pinterest is one of the growing social networking sites today. Pinterest works more like Instagram and it is a great site where people can share photos, ideas, and even dreams.

Big and small businesses alike use Pinterest to promote their product. Here are some of the most strategic ways that you can use Pinterest to market your products:

1. Create a Pinterest Board that will showcase your keywords.

The Pinterest Board is where you organize all your pins (things you have bookmarked). You can have a different board for different topics or categories. There are also Group Boards that only invited members can see.

You have to include your keywords in your Pinterest board. You see, Pinterest has an amazing search capability so take advantage of these capabilities by strategically placing your keywords in your Pinterest board title.

2. Use the Pin description to spread some valuable ideas.

Use the Pin description to share some valuable ideas to your followers. Remember that your followers can tweet your pin so make sure that your pin description is only 180 characters long.

Here are some of the tips that you can use in pinning a graphic:

- Add and brand your custom image to your website.
- Add 100 to 200 words to describe your image or your pin.
- Add the link to your home page or your blog article in your pin description.

3. Embed the pins on your blog.

Embedding pins on your blog site is really easy. It is also a great way to attract more followers and get more pins. You can actually create an Embed code on Pinterest, then incorporate this in the layout of your website. By embedding pins, more users will be able to re-pin and share your content.

4. Share your boards and pins on your other social networking sites.

It is best to tweet your pin and share these pins on social networking sites if these are relevant. This allows everyone who follow your other social media accounts to see your activity on Pinterest, which is especially important for those who do not have Pinterest accounts yet.

5. Get to know your audience.

Pinterest is largely used by the female population, mostly moms. Therefore, Pinterest is a great way to market products that are appealing to women, especially moms. If your customers are mostly men, it is not a wise decision to market your products on Pinterest.

Make sure that your photos also match the Pinterest aesthetic. These are images that are clear, crisp and well-composed. Minimalist and rustic styles are also very popular with users.

6. You have to take the content marketer hat and ditch the advertiser hat.

If you are planning to market your products on Pinterest, you have to be more of a content marketer and less of an advertiser. Pinterest users prefer engaging content and not some impersonal marketing pitch. Studies show that more than half of Pinterest users click on Pins that are linked to articles and blog posts. Most users like content that are useful or interesting in some way.

Topics that are popular in Pinterest are usually fashion, beauty, food, décor, and crafts. But, the good news is, it is okay even if your business is not related to these topics. All you need to do is find an image or content that is visually appealing to win "repins".

You can create boards that contain images from blog entries, infographics, and photos of staff members.

7. Identify your optimal pinning frequency.

Pinning excessively will definitely annoy or overwhelm your followers. But, pinning once every two months may make your Pinterest followers forget that you exist. So, it is best to create a pinning or posting schedule.

8. Create collaborative boards.

If you want to reach a new group of Pinterest users, it is best to create collaborative boards. This will also ensure that your pins are more visible to your target market.

Pinterest is a great way to market your product. It is also a great way to share ideas and learn new ideas that can help take your business to a whole new level.

# Chapter 6

# Using YouTube for Marketing

YouTube is one social media channel where you can market your products and services. Now that Google owns YouTube, you can also use YouTube for link building and Search Engine Optimization (SEO).

Here are some tips that you can use in using YouTube for marketing:

1. Create a YouTube channel.

The first step in using YouTube for marketing is to create a channel. This is where you can upload your videos. You have to make sure that your username reflects your brand.

There is an About section on your YouTube page where you can write about your business. This is where you can put important information about your company. It is also possible to include links to your social media accounts.

You can also categorize your videos into different sections like "Our Fans" or "Product Demonstrations". Creating playlists also has a similar function and helps users watch all your related videos without pausing.

2. Invest time in connecting with the other members of the YouTube community.

Place a comment on videos that are relevant to your business and always include the link to your YouTube channel or website in your comments. This will increase the traffic to your website and your channel. Try to reply to any questions and interesting comments from other users.

You can also ask viewers to like your video, comment and subscribe to your channel. You can put this request in the description of your videos or explicitly say it in your videos.

3. Always focus on brand recognition.

Making YouTube videos can increase brand recognition. But, if you want to reap these benefits, you have to include your company name or logo at the beginning or end of the video.

Try to have visual consistency among all your videos so that viewers can easily recognize a video as one of yours. It can be a similar background, using the same typography or the same voiceover. You can also have the same presenter or actor for all your videos. Make sure it is somebody quite charming and engaging. If you are comfortable on camera, then you can star in the videos yourself.

4. Use the right keywords.

You have to use the right keywords in formulating your video title and description. Ask yourself, what do customers type on YouTube to find products similar to mine? If you are selling ladies' bags, make sure to include that in your YouTube video title. You have to make sure that your content is related to your title. Write titles that catch people's attention. Do not just put "New Product by Company X" when you can put "Awesome Product that Would Change Your Life – Company X." The latter is more interesting and will definitely get a higher number of clicks.

5. Create valuable content.

To effectively use YouTube to market your products and services, you have to create a content that showcases your products and services. But, you have to create a video that pique the interest of your potential customers. Your videos must be engaging and interesting.

You can create "how to" videos or videos that showcases the unique feature of your products and services. You can also aim to create videos that you intend to go viral. These are usually humorous or clever videos that people want to "like" and share with their friends.

6. Post videos regularly.

If you are serious about using YouTube for your business, you have to post videos regularly. This will keep your customers and potential customers updated. Think of the videos on your YouTube channel as if they were shows on a TV channel. TV shows have a regular schedule that people know so they can tune in when their favorite shows are on. Make sure that people know the schedule when you upload new videos so they can log on to YouTube when that happens. You can also simply invite them to subscribe to your channel so that they get notified when you have new videos out.

You can reap a lot of benefits from using YouTube to market your products. YouTube is SEO-friendly and it's free. It is also a great way to give a "face" behind your amazing products and services. It is also a great way to demonstrate your expertise and establish yourself as an industry authority. Setup YouTube for your business and begin posting videos.

# Chapter 7

# Using Snapchat for Quick Marketing Tactics

Snapchat used to just be another photo and video sharing mobile application. Many people did not quite understand what made it better or more different than Instagram and Twitter that have similar functions. It seems to even be a more stripped down version of those apps and has limited capabilities. However, with more than 100 million users with an account on the app sharing 400 million snaps every day, Snapchat is a social media dark horse.

There is a limit on how long a photo or video can be viewed by an account's followers. This was its original selling point, so users can share a post that their friends will only see for a short time. It can be for mere seconds and it will not be seen again by the receiver. In essence, your message self-destructs. This poses a challenge for marketers, but they can also use it to their advantage if they know the following:

1. Create a Snapchat account.

As with your other social media accounts, you have to download the app and create an account. Follow the previously mentioned guidelines for usernames and profile photos.

2. Know your audience.

Snapchat's users are fairly young with most falling in the 18-34 year old age range. It also has a very casual tone. People just share quick snaps of what they are doing at the moment like their breakfast or a selfie. That is why you must settle for a fairly casual tone with your posts. Also, they must look fun and easy, so take advantage of the drawing function on the app to doodle or add stickers on your photos. This may be unacceptable for very serious, corporate businesses, but it will also show another side to their companies. Sharing videos is also useful for showing sneak peeks of an event or a product.

3. Do not feel constrained by the time limit.

You can look at the time limit as an opportunity to give teasers or short previews. Sometimes, people become more interested about a product if you do not give a lot of information about it right away. This creates buzz and speculation that will make people even more excited about what you will announce later on.

What marketers have to understand is that most of the content on all social media sites are viewed by users in five seconds or less, making them not any different from the experience of using Snapchat. It is also similar to the experience of passing a billboard on a fast moving highway or flipping to a TV channel and catching a few seconds of a commercial. However, the difference lies on not being able to find the content again while users can look back at old Tweets and Facebook timelines, so make sure that your posts are all memorable and easy to digest.

Take a cue from how other brands use Snapchat for advertising and think of many creative ways to use it for marketing. It is good to work with the time limit to create a sense of urgency so that customers will go and purchase the product immediately before it is too late.

## SOCIAL MEDIA

4. Engage with your followers.

You can come up with contests where people can send you photos or videos in relation to your business. This helps in increasing the purchase and use of your products and it allows you to interact with users.

5. Share exclusive, private content.

Snaps cannot be seen by people who are not following your account. So, your customers will feel special every time you deliver content that other people will not be able to see. It is more personal and intimate, which makes you connect better with customers.

You can also share promo codes or announcements about flash sales on Snapchat. That makes your users feel rewarded for following you on the app.

Similarly, you can bring people behind the scenes and let them see you at work - developing and delivering your products. This makes your customers feel like they are part of the company, too, in some way.

6. Find influencers you can partner with.

Find influencers like celebrities or social media stars who can promote your brand on Snapchat. They should have millions of followers and have an image that is related and relevant to your brand. You can ask them to post snaps while using your product or in your store.

7. Use Snapchat's advertising features.

As part of Snapchat's push to monetize the app, they are now allowing brands to use ad options. The first one is "Live Stories". Users can share photos and videos of an event live, so you can have a collection of snaps from different users who are present at a live event. For example, if there is a concert, then different people can show themselves, show the acts playing, or show the crowd to their friends via the app.

By looking at all the snaps together, users can get an idea about what is going on. In a way, they can also enjoy the event or even go there at that moment to catch the rest of it in person. Companies can pay for a 10-second spot to advertise in a live story. It is better if the live story is related to their business or actually sponsored by them.

Another ad option is "Discover". These are targeted ads that cost 2 cents for every view. You can buy these ad spaces from publishers or news outlets like ESPN or CNN. Budget for a certain number of views to be more cost-effective.

Take note that "Brand Story" is no longer offered by Snapchat. It is similar to sponsored ads on Twitter or Facebook where users can see ads from accounts that they are not following. Live Story is for people who are following the story while Discover is for people following the publisher's account.

Snapchat can be an intimidating and difficult to understand app at first, but once you integrate it into a concrete marketing plan, it can generate a lot of leads for you. Its brilliance lies in its simple and straightforward nature. It also fills the gap, which is missing in other social media platforms.

# Chapter 8

# Using Vine for Viral Marketing

Vine is a video sharing platform where users are limited to posting only six seconds of content that can be played in an endless loop. When using it for marketing, it works because of the short attention span of users and the entertainment value of the content. It is especially great for creating viral videos that people would like to share with others.

1. Create a Vine account.

Like with other social media apps, you have to download the app and create an account with a username and profile photo. Make sure that your Vine profile is consistent with your other social media accounts.

2. Make it memorable.

It is easy to forget a 6-second video, so many brands would come up with content that is useful or clever - important characteristics of viral content. For example, you can come up with a video demonstrating an unusual life hack using your product. Through good editing and composition, six seconds will be enough to convey an important message about your company.

3. Ask for user-generated content.

You can ask other users to make content for you featuring your products or service. This can be in the form of a contest with an exciting reward. Ask them to be creative and fun with their Vine videos.

4. Supplement Vine with other social media platforms.

As with other social media apps, you have to look at your entire social media marketing strategy. Using Vine alone will not generate a lot of leads for you, but if you promote your new uploads in your other accounts then more people will be able to see them. For users who are not active on Vine, you can make your Vine content accessible to them by creating video compilations on YouTube or republishing the videos on Instagram.

5. Use the app to show some personality.

You or your employees can be Vine stars, too. If it works with your brand, then you can show yourselves doing wacky videos or crazy stunts. Your products can also star in funny stop-motion or animated videos. Take into consideration, though, the casual tone of Vine. It is quite similar to Snapchat in the sense that content does not have to look perfect or overproduced.

Vine is a social media platform that is easy to disregard because it seems too simple, but it is one of the most effective ways to deliver viral content to numerous followers. Most of the time, viral marketing does not have to be complicated but it must give some form of value to consumers like entertainment or education.

# Chapter 9

## Using Blogs to Market your Product

Back in the day, blogs are mostly used to express personal feelings and musings. These days, it is a very effective tool to generate traffic for a website.

Using blogs for your business has many benefits:

1. Setting up a business blog will help drive traffic to your website.

Of course, everyone wants to have more website visitors. So, how does blog drive traffic to your site? Well, it is pretty simple. Your website probably does not have many pages and its content is not updated very frequently. Blogs solve both problems.

Every time you post a blog entry, it is considered as an additional indexed page on your website. It is a cue to search engines such as Google, Bing, and Yahoo that you have an active website. This is the reason why having a blog will help put you on page 1 of the search engines. And, if you are on page 1 for the keywords in your niche, it means that you will generate more traffic to your site.

For example, if you have an online dating site, adding blog entries about online dating may help put you on the number 1 spot of Google Search Results page when a client type in "online dating".

2. Setting up a business blog helps convert traffic into leads.

You can generate leads through your website by adding call to action buttons like free fact sheets, free ebooks, free trials, and free webinars. People love free downloadables that are helpful and useful to them. These can serve as free trials or act as supplements to your product or service. Doing so will entice customers to avail of your products and understand better what they can gain from patronizing your business.

3. Blogs help establish authority.

Writing good articles about your industry will help you establish your authority in that particular industry. You can share insights that you have gained throughout your experience in the industry and even give people advice or tips. Come out with good quality content that is informative.

Here are some tips that you can use in using blogs to promote and market your product:

- Build a strong foundation for your blog.

If you want your blog to be the center of your marketing plan, you have to make sure that your blog is built on a strong foundation.

You have to make sure that you have your own URL. Do not use free hosting options such as WordPress or Blogger. It is best to go for a self-hosted blog that WordPress offers. You also need to incorporate your blog into your main company website.

- Get to know your audience.

Before you start writing your blog, you have to know the people who will blog your blog. To do this, you have to create marketing personas. If you are targeting different and distinct audiences, it is important to create different marketing personas. It is also important to create more than one blog to cater to different audiences.

- Develop a strong marketing plan.

If you are going to walk down the content marketing road, you have to start planning your marketing events for the year. This will make it easier for you to determine what to blog about. You have to write about Tradeshows and conferences that your company will take part of. You need to plan your content carefully.

- Make sure that your blog content reflects your brand and your company.

You have to make sure that it is easy for readers to associate the blog content with your product, brand, or company.

It is also important to break down your content into bullet points. This will make it easier for your readers to process information.

- Write about the big 7.

You have to take advantage of the big 7 content strategies:

- Promote your services and products.
- You need to position yourself as an industry expert.
- Announce launches or new products.
- Share amazing and flattering stories about your products, your brand, and your company.

- You need to write a content that answers frequently asked questions about your product.

- You need to create blog posts about your accomplishments and milestones.

- You also need to write about job openings in your company.

- Plant keywords into your blog post.

- As mentioned earlier in this chapter, blog posts can help you with Search Engine Optimization or SEO. If you are targeting certain keywords in your niche, you have to strategically place those keywords on your blog post.

- Link your blog post to other blogs.

- When you see a blog that you find interesting, comment on that post and make sure to post backlinks to your blog or your website. This is one way to improve your site or blog traffic.

- Integrate your blog to your other social networking accounts.

You need to link your blog to your other accounts such as Twitter and Facebook. Post a link of your blog on your Facebook account or tweet about it.

Creating and maintaining blogs is one of the cheapest ways to promote your product and improve your online presence. It is also a great way to share your stories and your ideas.

# Conclusion

Thank you again for purchasing this book!

I hope this book was able to help you learn more about social media marketing!

The next step is to put this information to use, and using the tips contained in this book! By applying the effective strategies and techniques you learned in this book you can create a strong social media brand presence for yourself and your business.

If you received value from this book, then I'd like to ask you a favor. Would you be kind enough to leave a review for this book on Amazon.

I want to reach as many people as I can with this book, and the more reviews will help me accomplish that!

Not only that you will get some good karma as well.

Thank you for your time. I wish you the best of luck.

Richard

www.ingramcontent.com/pod-product-compliance
Lightning Source LLC
Chambersburg PA
CBHW060417190526
45169CB00002B/937